ALCO'S
TO ALLENTOWN

BY THOMAS A. BIERY

The Railroad Press

1150 Carlisle Street, Suite 444
Hanover, PA 17331-1100

Printed in the United States of America by HBP, Hagerstown, Maryland.
Color by GGS, York, Pennsylvania.

International Standard Book Number 0-9657709-1-5

The Railroad Press
Publishers of:

TRP Magazine

*CF7 Locomotives:
From Cleburne to
Everywhere*

ALCO'S TO ALLENTOWN

BY THOMAS A. BIERY

THE HISTORIC LEHIGH RIVER VALLEY...5

A TRIP AROUND THE VALLEY...16

TRAIN WATCHING IN THE 1960'S...99

MOTIVE POWER...104

CNJ and Reading Company power idle beneath the old coaling tower at the Bethlehem Engine Terminal in 1967. A CNJ snowplow is hiding in the underbrush surrounding the Jim Thorpe turntable in 1969.

Foreword

The medium of photography allows us to see through the eyes of the photographer. This personal album of my Kodachrome and black & white photos will transport you back to the Lehigh Valley of the 1960's. My interest in railroad photography was fueled by books and magazines. The camera that I used to take the photographs was primitive compared to the computer controlled equipment that I currently own. The railroads and locations photographed have also changed, so much so that they would not be recognized today. Many of the railroad lines were abandoned years ago. It is not my intention to lament the passing of the anthracite railroads, but rather to share with you the wonder and excitement of the trains that passed in front of my camera. I was told early on that a photographer would always carry a camera everywhere and capture the world around him or her. My camera was at my side and I took the picture even when others challenged my intent.

Railroading is still fascinating to me and I continue to carry a camera to record the moment. The young railfans that I meet today express the same excitement and wonder about this hobby as I did in my youth. It is to them that I dedicate this book.

Tom Biery
Cumberland, Maryland
April 1998

THE HISTORIC
LEHIGH RIVER VALLEY

A brakeman climbs aboard lead GP30 3605 in the Allentown Yard. The trainline air has been pumped up and departure for Reading is near. As long as Bethlehem Steel would be in business, coal and other mineral trains were frequently coming and going around the clock.

llentown has long been the center of economic activity in eastern Pennsylvania. Located only 100 miles west of New York City and 70 miles north of Philadelphia, Allentown is often overlooked as a major city on the Eastern seaboard. The Allentown-Bethlehem-Easton metropolitan area census is nearing 610,000 residents as the new millennia approaches. Today this dynamic metroplex is a major distribution center serving the vast population centers of the northeast. A-B-E International airport is just minutes from downtown Allentown and Bethlehem. Allentown is also located on the shortest land route between the Port of New York and the West; Interstate 78, a major trucking route, passes through the area on a direct route to New York City, and Conrail east-west freight trains run through Allentown en route to New York City, bypassing the old Pennsylvania Railroad route through Philadelphia.

Philadelphia became a main port of entry for European immigration to Pennsylvania during the 19th century. The new arrivals moved north and west from Philadelphia looking for cheap land. The land

east of the Appalachian Mountains was very fertile and the new immigrants established a rural farming economy. They cleared the land of trees, tended to their animal herds and developed communities in the area we now call the Lehigh Valley.

Small iron furnaces operating along the Schuylkill River near Philadelphia relied on Virginia soft coal for smelting. The British blockade during the War of 1812 cut off this supply of bituminous and forced the owners to look elsewhere for fuel. The U.S. Government was in desperate need of iron for munitions and ship building. With fuel in short supply they would try to use local hard coal from eastern Pennsylvania. The anthracite was difficult to ignite and burned slower than bituminous. However, the ironmasters soon learned to use the black rock by applying a steady bottom draft of air. Small amounts of hard coal were delivered to Josiah White and Erskine Hazard who owned an iron works at the Falls of the Schuylkill near Philadelphia. The ironmasters were successful in using the new fuel and would turn their attention to the construction of a canal for its transport. Soon eastern Pennsylvania would establish

Cool morning air blows through the open doors of Ironton Railroad 8. In a few moments number 8 will be coupled to Baldwin locomotive 751, seen in the distance. The little railroad was primarily responsible for servicing cement mills at Coplay, Egypt, and Ormrod.

itself as a leader in the production of pig and wrought iron with Anthracite coal.

The demand for anthracite increased rapidly and fueled the American Industrial Revolution. The coalfields north of Allentown at Summit Hill were easy to mine and the coal burned very hot with little ash. It would make an excellent fuel for iron production. A canal was constructed along the Lehigh River between White Haven and Easton to transport the coal to eastern markets. The Lehigh Canal, charted in 1818 would remain in operation for the next 118 years. A gravity railroad was also constructed between the mine at Summit Hill and the Lehigh River at Mauch Chunk. From Easton the coal boats traversed the Delaware Canal to Philadelphia and the Morris canal to New York markets.

An act of the Pennsylvania Legislature gave control of the Lehigh River to the Lehigh Navigation Company in 1818. They were excellent businessmen; owning both coal mines and a canal, the Lehigh Coal

and Lehigh Navigation Company marketed the Lehigh Canal and the potential waterpower available from each slackwater dam erected along the Lehigh River. Josiah White and Erskine Hazard, principal owners of the Lehigh Coal and Navigation Company (name after 1820) offered free water rights to any person erecting and operating an iron furnace between Hokendauqua and Allentown.

The challenge to build an iron furnace was accepted by David Thomas of Wales. He constructed his Lehigh Crane Iron Company at Biery's Port (Catasauqua). The eight foot drop of the Lehigh River at Lock 36 was used to power the blast furnace bellows. By 1840 the iron furnace was in operation and the town was renamed Craneville in 1844, only later to be changed again in 1846 to Catasauqua. The iron ore was obtained on the west side of the Lehigh River in Upper Macungie and South Whitehall townships. The ore was delivered by horse and wagon teams over a crude roadway. In 1857 the Catasauqua & Fogelsville Railroad was constructed to replace the wagon delivery system. The success of the Lehigh Crane Iron Company prompted other entrepreneurs to build iron furnaces in Coplay, Hokendauqua, Allentown, Bethlehem, Easton and Phillipsburg, NJ.

The Ironton Railroad Company was constructed between Hokendauqua, site of the Thomas Iron Company works and the hematite iron ore quarries at Ironton, a distance of five and a half miles. The line later reached Orefield and Siegersville in 1862. An extension to Coplay was built to serve an infant cement industry.

Improvements in technology near the end of the 19th century eventually forced the demise of smaller furnaces in the Lehigh Valley. By using updated equipment and technology the Bethlehem Iron Company emerged from the 19th century as a world leader in the production of iron and steel.

A symbiotic relationship developed between the Lehigh Valley Railroad Company and Bethlehem Iron Company. Lehigh Valley Railroad president Asa Packer and superintendent Robert Sayre were board members of the company. Together they called on John Fritz of the Cambria Iron Works to bring his expertise to Bethlehem. His immediate job was to rebuild the ironworks with a new three-high rolling mill for the production of iron rails. The Lehigh Valley Railroad Co. was in dire need of quality American-made iron rails. By 1873 the Bethlehem Iron Company was producing steel rails with the new Bessemer converter process.

Soon the new mill came to the attention of the U.S. government. The U.S. Navy was about to embark on the construction of the great white fleet and the bid went to Bethlehem. An enlarged mill provided propeller shafts, armor plating and large caliber guns for the new battleships.

Other capital improvements would result in construction of the Grey Mill (named after its inventor Henry Grey) designed to produce 48 inch wide I-beams for bridges and skyscrapers. The Golden Gate Bridge in San Francisco, George Washington Bridge in New York City, and Ben Franklin Bridge in Philadelphia were constructed with I-beams from Bethlehem. Add

A GP7, Train Master and a GP30 are ready to depart Allentown for Lurgan with empty hoppers to be refilled for The Steel. Reading was a vital link between Bethlehem Steel and the eastern bituminous coalfields via their connection with the WM.

the Empire State Building, Waldorf-Astoria Hotel, and Chrysler Building to the list of well-known buildings constructed around skeletons of Bethlehem-produced steel.

The amount of raw materials delivered to the mill and finished product shipped out by railroad was staggering! The firm's name was changed to Bethlehem Steel Company in 1899. Handling the tremendous quantities of raw materials and finished product at the Bethlehem plant resulted in construction of a special switching railroad. Incorporated 1910, the Philadelphia, Bethlehem and New England Railroad Company serviced the steel plant, United Gas Improvement Company and coke works. The line interchanged with Lehigh Valley Railroad Company, Reading Company and Central Railroad Company of New Jersey.

During the later half of the 19th century railroad construction accelerated along the Lehigh River. Prompted by the monopolistic pricing practices of the canal operators, a fledgling railroad industry began to emerge along the Lehigh River. The Central of New Jersey reached Phillipsburg, New Jersey, from the east in 1852. It would transport coal from the Lehigh Canal at Phillipsburg to New York City via rail. About the same time the Lehigh Valley was constructing a line along the west bank of the Lehigh River between Mauch Chunk and Easton. Trains began operating through Allentown in 1855.

The East Pennsylvania Railroad completed a line between Reading and Allentown in 1859. It connected with the Lehigh Valley at East Penn Junction. The line was leased to the Philadelphia and Reading Railroad Company in 1869. Coal could now be transported via railroad between the coal fields and New York City and Philadelphia. Philadelphia was reached via the Belvidere Delaware Railroad operating between Phillipsburg and Trenton following the Delaware River's east bank. Soon the North Penn Railroad opened a direct overland route between Philadelphia and Bethlehem.

Not to be outdone, the Lehigh Coal & Navigation Co. completed their own Lehigh & Susquehanna Railroad in 1867. It paralleled their canal on the east bank of the Lehigh River. In 1871 the Central Railroad of New Jersey leased the L&S, giving the CNJ a continuous railroad between Jersey City and

Wilkes-Barre. The Lehigh Coal & Navigation Co. gained control of Lehigh and New England Railroad Company in 1904. The line was eventually expanded through acquisitions and new right of way. By 1918 L&NE trains were carrying coal to eastern New York and New England via a connection with the New Haven at Maybrook, New York. Branches were extended to Allentown, Bethlehem, and Catasauqua all via Crane Junction near Bath.

The Lehigh Valley Railroad was very successful and soon expanded east and west. The mainline was completed to Waverly, New York, in 1869, and a third rail was laid on the Erie Railroad (6 foot gauge) to Buffalo. The LV immediately acquired the Tifft farm south of Buffalo and began building its own terminal and lakefront facilities, twenty five years before it would enter Buffalo on its own rails! It completed a line to New York Harbor from Phillipsburg in 1875. Extensive pier facilities were constructed on Black Tom Island in Jersey City. The last great construction project was completion of its mainline to Buffalo in 1892. It was the last of the "Great Lakes to the sea" railroads and also the longest... the Delaware, Lackawanna & Western route was 50 miles shorter.

By the end of the 19th century the majority of railroad lines which would survive until Conrail's inception were in place. Other railroads such as the L&NE would not survive the onslaught of motor truck competition and the decline of Anthracite shipments.

During construction of the Lehigh Canal, rock suitable for making natural hydraulic cement was discovered at Northampton. About 1830 the Lehigh Coal and Navigation Company constructed a cement mill consisting of four kilns near the site. The limestone rock was crushed with burr mill stones and the plant produced ten barrels of cement per day. The cement was used in building locks for the new canal. Forty years later in nearby Coplay, David Saylor received a patent for the production of Portland cement. This publicity sparked a boom in the cement industry. The original plant at Siegfried (Northampton) was acquired by The Lawrence Portland Cement Company and production began in 1889. Keystone Cement Company began production with its new rotary kilns at Coplay that same year.

The largest cement manufacturing venture was established in Northampton in 1895. The Atlas Cement

Lehigh Water Gap at Blue Mountain has provided spectacular vistas for travelers since the Lenni Lenape Indians hunted along the banks of the Lehigh River. The Lehigh & New England's celebrated bridge over the Lehigh was dismantled after the L&NE closed their doors for good. The bridge carried trains high over the CNJ and LV while crossing from the east side of the Lehigh Gap to the west. This was part of their mainline linking the coal fields around Tamaqua with New England. The view at left faces west from the east bank of the river. The photo below looks south along the CNJ mainline.

Two ALCO roadswitchers bring a local train into Cementon on a lazy Spring day in 1966.

Company constructed three large cement plants on 763 acres of land between Hokendauqua Creek and Northampton Borough. The vast expansion of the cement industry brought thousands of new immigrants from Europe. The Atlas alone provided 8 million barrels of cement required to construct locks for the Panama Canal. During the 1920's three quarries and 71 kilns operating around the clock produced 200 carloads of product daily. More than 5000 people were employed. A company railroad was constructed in 1896 to handle transport of coal to, and cement from, the huge cement plant. The Northampton and Bath Railroad Company built to a connection with the Central Railroad of New Jersey in Northampton. More than a dozen cement plants located in Lehigh and Northampton counties were producing cement by World War I. Northampton was located in the center of the world's largest concentration of cement manufacturing plants.

One of the later railroads to operate from the Lehigh River valley was Chestnut Ridge RR Co. Opened in 1900 from a connection with the CNJ at Palmerton, the line originally serviced a brick kiln at Kunkletown ten and one half miles east. After bankruptcy, it was renamed Chestnut Ridge Railway and purchased by the New Jersey Zinc Co. in 1907. The mainline was extended to connect the sprawling zinc works and the company's own internal switching trackage.

The industrial might of the Lehigh River valley was evident throughout the first half of the 20th century. Production of steel centered in the city of Bethlehem. Bethlehem Steel was transformed into the second largest steel producer in the United States. Cement production increased throughout Lehigh and Northampton counties. The world's largest single cement mill, Atlas Cement Company, was located in Northampton. By 1900 the Lehigh Valley was producing 70 percent of the cement made in the United States. Dozens of clothing, shoe, and textile factories were developed with hundreds of workers in each. There was also food processing -- flour, meat, candy, and beer were all produced locally. Machine parts, paper products, paint and electrical components filled thousands of box cars. In 1905 the Mack brothers began production of truck, bus and fire apparatus in Allentown. A vast railroad network was constructed into many small towns to serve farmers, industrialists, and merchants.

The end of World War II brought about great changes to the transportation system nationally and locally. A love affair with the automobile began; a populace once satisfied with walking to work or using the trolley and train found new freedom in automobile ownership. Factories built during WWII were now retooled to produce affordable automobiles. Military truck production was changed overnight to produce vehicles for domestic use. A new, more modern highway system began to develop nationwide and in the Lehigh Valley. By the late 1950's, four-lane Route 22 was constructed between New York City, Easton, Bethlehem, and Harrisburg, replacing a narrow two lane road. The Pennsylvania Turnpike was expanded north from Philadelphia, passing Allentown on the west side on its route to Scranton.

Railroads were facing a critical challenge to their very survival. A decline of anthracite car loadings after the Korean War was only the beginning of trouble for rail lines serving the region. The Pennsylvania PUC made a major decision in 1959 to allow truck delivery of cement from local Lehigh Valley plants. Prior to this time railroads enjoyed a monopoly on this lucrative traffic. The era of big trucks had begun.

The first victim of the PUC decision was abandonment of a major portion of the Lehigh and New England Railroad by the owner Lehigh Coal and Navigation Co. The L&NE ceased operations on October 31, 1961. The CNJ purchased trackage to Allentown, Bethlehem, Bath, Martins Creek, Hauto and Tamaqua. Erie-Lackawanna purchased Wind Gap to Pen Argyl trackage.

The Lehigh Valley Railroad abandoned the remainder of their passenger service by Feb. 8, 1961. A 106 year history of passenger operations was silenced by a mix of airplane, bus and private car. During the early 1960's, passenger service in the Lehigh Valley was reduced to CNJ's Allentown to Jersey City service and Reading Co.'s passenger trains from Allentown to Harrisburg and Bethlehem to Philadelphia.

ALCO PA1's 610 and 601 accelerate east with freshly produced bulk cement from the busy Whitehall Cement Company. The banked curve at Cementon is good for 60mph, as is much of the track on the Lehigh Valley RR mainline to Packerton.

A decline in freight traffic caused great changes to occur. By 1965, much of the multiple-track Lehigh Valley Railroad was reduced to a CTC'd single track railroad. The CNJ was on the brink of bankruptcy at the same time and drastic measures were taken to reduce operating costs. An agreement was drawn-up in which the LV and CNJ would share operation of CNJ's Allentown Yard. In addition, duplicate trackage would be eliminated between Easton and Wilkes-Barre. Even this was not enough to save the CNJ... they eventually declared bankruptcy in 1967.

On February 1, 1968, the largest railroad merger in United States history took place. The Pennsy and New York Central were merged into Penn Central Company. Two years later, the giant Penn Central, with 20,000 miles of track, 95,000 employees and assets of $4.5 billion, would become the largest corporate bankruptcy in U.S. history. The Lehigh Valley Railroad, controlled by the Penn Central, declared bankruptcy three days later, on June 24, 1970. By 1971 the Reading Company joined the growing club of bankrupt lines.

The bankruptcy was financially devastating to the United States economy. A U.S. government corporation, the United States Railway Association, was incorporated to save the railroad. From the smoldering wreckage of the giant Penn Central and six other regional railroad properties was formed the Consolidated Rail Corporation - Conrail. Railroads included in Conrail were Penn Central, Central Railroad of New Jersey, Erie-Lackawanna, Lehigh Valley, Reading Company, Lehigh and Hudson River and other subsidiary roads, including the famous Pennsylvania-Reading Seashore Lines, owned jointly by the PRR and the Reading.

With a huge infusion of Federal money, the new corporation immediately began to rationalize its physical plant. Important mainlines like the Pennsylvania Railroad through Altoona and the New York Central through Buffalo were saved and improved. Other mainlines, such as the Lehigh Valley Railroad through New York state, were abandoned. The last railroad to build a line into Buffalo from the East Coast would be the first to go.

A light rain is falling as a Burro crane and gondola head west through Laury's Station. A once mighty Lehigh Valley Railroad boasted four main tracks here. The weather isn't the only thing that's gloomy.

1960's Photography

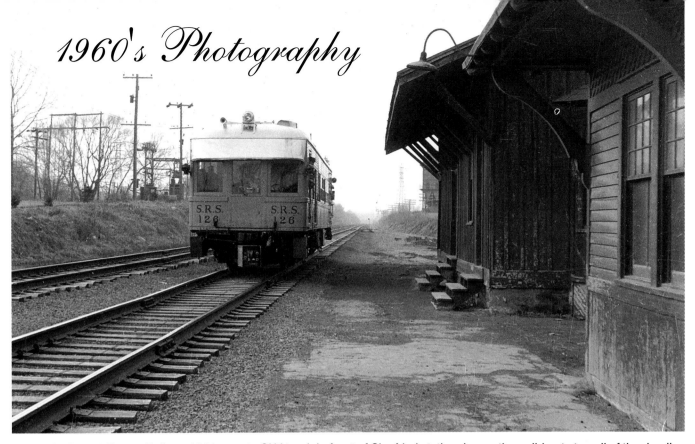

During April 1963 Sperry Rail car 126 inspects CNJ track in front of Siegfried station. Inspections did not stop all of the derailments -- the tracks on both sides of the river between Allentown and Mauch Chunk are infamous for their spectacular wrecks.

The photographs in this book were taken with three different 35mm cameras. My first camera, a Kodak PONY IV, was given to me as a gift for my 12th birthday. It was a small compact all-manual camera with a 44mm f3.5 Kodak Anastar Lens. The shutter was cocked manually and exposure set with a separate Sekonic light meter. The pictures were acceptable, but not fantastic. In 1964 I purchased a used Voigtlander Bessematic SLR for $40.00. This West German camera had a superb F2.8 50mm Color Skopar lens and built in light meter coupled to the Syncro-Compur shutter. Kodachromes taken with this camera were very sharp and rich in color and contrast. The shutter failed during my senior year in high school. It was cheaper to replace the camera than repair it. The replacement was a Praktica Nova B manufactured in East Germany. The quality of the camera was questionable but the Carl Zeiss Jena f2.8 50mm lens was outstanding. The photographs taken between 1966 and 1970 were made with the Praktica. The East German Zeiss lens produced rich and contrasty photographs. I added a Vivitar f2.8 135mm to the arsenal in 1967. The Lehigh Valley set of A-B-B-A F's at Slatington was photographed with the 135mm. It was a cheap but effective telephoto lens.

The film selection was simple. Kodak Plus-X for black and white photos and Kodachrome for color transparencies. On rare occasions Ektachrome (ASA 32) was used when more speed was required. By the mid '60's Kodak introduced Kodachrome II with an ASA of 25. It produced wonderful saturated color with double the speed of the original Kodachrome (ASA10). I chose Kodak processing for Kodachrome and Ektachrome film. The Kodachromes are still vivid after 35 years while the Ektachrome dyes are beginning to fade. Kodachrome is unique because the color dyes are added at the lab. This process can only be done with an elaborate and expensive processing machine. Other transparency films have the color couplers built into the emulsion, allowing for easy and quick processing. Time has proven the stability and longevity of Kodachrome. E-6 color films produced today are much more stable and the colors will remain true for many years if properly cared for.

The black and white photographs were exposed on Kodak Plus-X (ASA125). The film was processed at home with Kodak Microdol-X developer. My teenage processing abilities were very amateur and some negatives are very dense. They were reprinted with a Besseler 35 Printmaker and El Nikkor 50mm f4 lens on Ilford Multigrade IV RC Deluxe resin coated base paper and developed in Dektol. My darkroom skills were developed as a member of the Northampton High School Photo Club.

LEHIGH VALLEY MAIN LINE
PHILLIPSBURG TO JIM THORPE
DISTANCE FROM NEW YORK

76.3	PHILLIPSBURG
76.6	PA.-N.J. STATE LINE
77.0	EASTON
77.8	SO. EASTON
77.9	ABBOTT
78.6	GLENDON
80.7	RICHARDS
83.0	REDINGTON
85.8	FREEMANSBURG
86.1	FLORENCE YARD
88.6	BETHLEHEM
90.7	GEISINGERS
92.5	EAST PENN JCT.
93.3	ALLENTOWN
95.0	GAP JCT.
96.0	FULLERTON
97.0	CATASAUQUA
99.0	COPLAY
100.3	CEMENTON
102.7	LAURYS
104.2	TREICHLER
109.5	SLATINGTON
111.4	LEHIGH GAP
114.9	LIZARD CREEK
115.7	BOWMANSTOWN
117.7	MAHONING
119.3	LEHIGHTON
121.3	PACKERTON JCT.
122.7	JIM THORPE

EASTON & NORTHERN BRANCH
EASTON TO BELFAST JCT.
DISTANCE FROM EASTON

0.0	EASTON
3.2	ALTA
4.3	18TH STREET
4.8	13TH STREET JCT.
9.1	TATAMY
9.8	L&NE JCT.
10.1	STOCKERTOWN
11.1	BELFAST JCT.

E-L BANGOR & PORTLAND BRANCH
PORTLAND TO BATH JCT.
DISTANCE FROM HOBOKEN

82.57	PORTLAND
89.84	BANGOR SHOPS
92.38	MARTINS CREEK JCT.
96.08	MARTINS CREEK, PA.
96.98	MARTINS CREEK N.J.
96.74	PEN ARGYL JCT.
97.24	PEN ARGYL
99.24	WIND GAP
103.58	BELFAST JCT.
103.80	HERCULES JCT.
106.74	NAZARETH
110.49	BATH JCT.

NORTHAMPTON & BATH RAILROAD
NORTHAMPTON TO BATH JCT.
DISTANCE FROM NORTHAMPTON

0.00	NORTHAMPTON
0.66	NAVARRO
2.68	WEAVERSVILLE
4.57	LERCHS
5.20	JACKSONVILLE
6.56	BATH
7.28	BATH JUNCTION

READING CO. BETHLEHEM BRANCH
BETHLEHEM TO TELFORD
DISTANCE FROM READING TERMINAL

56.6	BETHLEHEM
56.5	WEST THIRD ST.
55.7	EAST THIRD ST.
54.3	LEHIGH
52.6	HELLERTOWN
47.6	CENTRE VALLEY
44.8	HILLTOP
40.2	QUAKERTOWN
37.2	ROCKHILL
35.5	KASIE
35.0	PERKASIE
33.6	SELLERSVILLE
30.9	TELFORD

EAST PENNSYLVANIA BRANCH
ALLENTOWN TO ALBURTIS
DISTANCE FROM ALLENTOWN

0.0	ALLENTOWN
0.4	"J" TOWER
0.5	EAST PENN JCT.
4.1	EMMAUS JCT.
5.7	EMMAUS
9.2	MACUNGIE
11.8	ALBURTIS

C&F BRANCH
CATASAUQUA TO ALBURTIS
DISTANCE FROM CATASAUQUA

0.0	CATASAUQUA
1.4	MICKLEY'S
2.5	SEIPLE
6.3	WALBERT
8.5	CHAPMAN
11.1	TREXLERTOWN
14.1	ALBURTIS

L&NE RAILROAD CO.
HAUTO TO PORTLAND
DISTANCE FROM HAUTO

0.7	HAUTO SCALE
0.4	S.C. BOOTH
0.0	HAUTO
1.1	WE 2 MAIN TRACKS
1.2	LANSFORD
1.4	TUNNEL JCT.
2.0	COALDALE
4.0	ROCK CUT EE 2 MAIN
4.9	ARLINGTON
5.3	GREENWOOD JCT.
6.1	TAMAQUA
7.4	PIONEER SIDING
12.1	CHAIN
21.3	ANDREAS
27.8	SEMMEL SIDING
28.6	SEMMEL
32.3	GAP JCT.
33.5	PALMERTON
34.7	BERLINSVILLE
37.4	DANIELSVILLE SIDING
38.1	DANIELSVILLE
45.6	BENDERS JCT.
48.7	HORN SPRINGS
52.5	PEN ARGYL SHOPS
53.7	PEN ARGYL
55.4	BANGOR JCT.
57.2	BANGOR
58.1	NORTH BANGOR
59.5	QUARRY JCT. SIDING
63.6	PORTLAND

CNJ MAIN LINE
PHILLIPSBURG TO PQ
DISTANCE FROM JERSEY CITY

72.12	PHILLIPSBURG
72.49	L&H. JUNCTION
72.77	EASTON
77.15	E.&W. JUNCTION
81.37	FREEMANSBURG
84.26	BETHLEHEM
84.50	"JU" INTERLOCKING
85.47	"STEEL" INTERLOCKING
87.00	"VN" INTERLOCKING
88.18	"R" INTERLOCKING
88.78	EAST ALLENTOWN
89.33	ALLENTOWN A.T.R.R.
90.20	"WK" INTERLOCKING
92.45	CATASAUQUA
94.48	NORTHAMPTON
102.45	LOCKPORT
108.11	PALMERTON
108.42	"HX" INTERLOCKING
110.05	WEST END HAZARD
117.79	JIM THORPE
119.18	NESQUEHONING JCT.

CNJ NESQUEHONING VALLEY BR.
PACKERTON JCT. TO TAMANEND
FROM NESQUEHONING JCT.

0.00	NESQUEHONING JCT.
3.44	NESQUEHONING
7.54	HAUTO
15.46	HAUCKS
16.72	TAMANEND

L&NE RAILROAD CO.
LEHIGH AND LACKAWANNA BR.
BENDERS JCT. TO BETH. JCT
DISTANCE FROM BENDERS JCT.

0.0	BENDERS JCT.
1.2	POINT PHILLIP
1.9	SUMMIT NEW SIDING
2.0	SUMMIT SIDING
2.1	SUMMIT
4.6	CHAPMAN QUARRIES SID.
7.1	BATH
8.4	CRANE JCT.
14.5	CATASAUQUA
11.6	NATIONAL SIDING
12.4	BRODHEAD
14.7	STOKE PARK SIDING
17.8	ALLEN JCT.
22.6	ALLENTOWN
18.8	BETHLEHEM
19.1	BETHLEHEM JCT.

L&NE RAILROAD CO. NAZARETH BR.
BATH TO MARTINS CREEK
DISTANCE FROM BATH

0.0	BATH
0.2	EE 2 MAIN TRACKS
2.4	TADMOR
2.8	WE 2 MAIN TRACKS
3.8	DEXTER TOWER
4.5	NAZARETH
8.4	STOCKERTOWN
12.4	PAXINOSA SIDING
15.5	SANDTS EDDY
16.9	MARTINS CREEK

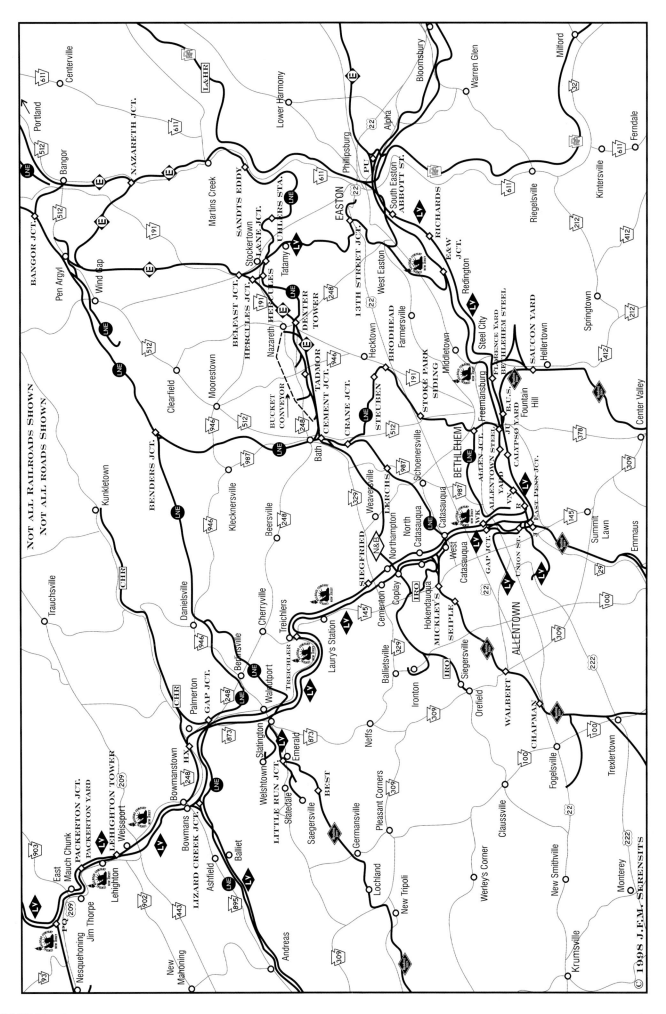

© 1998 J.F.M. SERENSITS

A Trip Around
The Valley

Climb aboard for a trip up and down the Lehigh River valley. We will begin at the confluence of the Lehigh and Delaware Rivers, where the CNJ and the LVRR cross from New Jersey into Pennsylvania. We will travel along the LV main through Bethlehem to Allentown's East Penn Junction, where everything came together! The Reading, CNJ and Lehigh Valley all met here in a complicated maze of trackage. We will visit the Allentown passenger stations and see Hokendauqua, Cementon and Laurys on our way to Lehighton's Packerton Yard. We will briefly stop at CNJ's Jim Thorpe (Mauch Chunk) facilities before heading back down the Central. We will squeeze

through Lehigh Gap, along with Lehigh & New England RR, Lehigh Valley RR and a 4-lane can-tilevered highway. We'll visit Treichler and Northampton on our way to the massive Allentown yard. We will sample some of the motive power at Bethlehem Engine Terminal and look at some of the happenings in the Allentown yard before exiting the east end at Bethlehem Junction's JU tower.

Along the way we will visit some smaller operations with interesting equipment and facilities, in order to give you a better understanding of what it was like if you were lucky enough to railfan the Lehigh Valley area in the 1960's and early 1970's.

Unique Lehigh Valley Ford Econoline maintenance of way vehicle heads west on track 1 at Bethlehem. The Reading Company "Bethlehem Branch" to Philadelphia meets the LVRR main here. The Hill to Hill bridge is adorned with Christmas trees.

Two Lehigh Valley C628 Snowbirds ease across the Delaware River bridge between Easton and Phillipsburg late in 1968. From here to Musconetcong Tunnel is an eleven mile climb of 0.4 to 0.9% easily handled by the big ALCO's. Conrail abandoned the Lehigh Valley bridge in favor of the Central of New Jersey span.

The Central of New Jersey station at Easton was a beautiful brick structure and included a large tower. The baggage carts are still available for use over the wooden platforms in this late Summer 1966 photo. The structure would later succumb to fire.

A number of railroads were within walking distance of CNJ's PU Tower in March 1966.
In addition to the CNJ were Erie-Lackawanna, LVRR, Lehigh & Hudson River and PRR.
The old Lackawanna freight station was located directly behind PU Tower on Market St.

A close examination of the Delaware River at Easton -
Phillipsburg in 1969 reveals two active bridges and
stone piers from an earlier CNJ bridge that still carried
track 3 until 1949. The bridge on the left belongs to the
Lehigh Valley Railroad, and was later abandoned by
Conrail in favor of the newer CNJ span on the right.

SW9 number 289 and twin are seen at the South Easton engine facility in July 1967. The 289 was traded to GE in 1974 after more than two decades of service. GE then sold the unit to the Youngstown and Northern.

A westbound is stopped at Abbott Street interlocking in South Easton so the crew can get instructions on the telephone. Today's power consists of an F7A, two EMD boosters and a high hood ALCO RS11.

The Pennsylvania Railroad served Phillipsburg by way of its Delaware River line from Trenton. When this photo was taken during Summer 1966, the motive power in this interesting yard was all ALCO. Steam power was long gone, but the facilities to service it were still visible.

ALCO T6 switcher number 9849 is seen at Phillipsburg, New Jersey, in Spring 1968. Last of five built for PRR, the locomotives were rated at 1000HP.

A short local freight rumbles past Easton station after crossing the Delaware River from Phillipsburg, New Jersey, late in 1969. LV 140 is a Baldwin DS4-4-1000, a switcher noted for its pulling ability.

Lehigh Valley dining cars were provisioned from this building in Easton. View is looking east toward Phillipsburg toward the end of Summer, 1969.

Mainline tracks 3 and 4, along with Calypso Yard, have been pulled up. Two RS11's and a Geep are setting out a Burlington and an Erie boxcar. They will finish up by returning to their train parked on westbound track number 1. The Hill to Hill bridge is in the background.

Rationalization along the LVRR at Bethlehem is in full swing as of July 1967. Little remains of once-busy Calypso Yard at mile marker 89 on the west side of Bethlehem. Work performed at Calypso was transferred to CNJ's Allentown yard in 1965. The engineer on the lead ALCO RS11 relies on hand signals to make a safe set out on a hot and steamy July 1967 morning.

The Reading and Lehigh Valley made use of bridges over the Lehigh River at each end of CNJ's Allentown Yard. At the east end of the yard, two Lehigh Valley ALCO roadswitchers rumble across the Lehigh River at Bethlehem. On the south (east) side of the bridge, the original through-truss was replaced with a wider girder bridge, here framed by the Hill to Hill bridge, to accommodate the new 1965 connection with the LV. This connection allowed direct access by LV trains from the east.

Children spend a lazy July 1967 day fishing from the pier of Allentown Terminal Railroad Company's Lehigh River bridge. Overhead an afternoon manifest freight pulls out of the west end of CNJ's Allentown Yard, headed for Macungie, Alburtis, Reading and beyond.

A Baldwin AS-16 will depart for Philadelphia with two PRR boxcars and a handful of coaches from Reading's Bethlehem Passenger station on a quiet Sunday late in 1962. There is litter on the tracks, but the platform has been swept clean. Note the coachyard to the left of 561 and the Hill to Hill bridge in the background above the train.

Iron ore destined for Bethlehem Steel has crested the 1.2% grade at Telford early in 1974. This overhead view from Route 309 gives a good idea of the limited amount of the extremely heavy iron ore loaded into each hopper car.

A Reading GP35/GP30 combo strains to get its train up and over the Lehigh River and LVRR mainline. Summer 1969.

An ALCO Century duo leads a westbound through torn-up East Penn Yard. Lead C630 number 5311 is lettered for "Bee Line Service" and is rated at 3000HP. She sports High-Adhesion trucks and a snow plow. Trailing C424 5204 is rated 2400HP. In the Summer of 1968, when this photo was taken, American Locomotive Works was just one year away from being history.

An RS3 and RS2 make easy work of the transfer run from Calypso Yard in Bethlehem, and begin working the interchange yard at East Penn Junction. A mix of semaphore and target signals date this late Spring 1966 photograph.

ALCO'S TO ALLENTOWN

CNJ eastbound passenger train accelerates for the steep climb to clear the LVRR mainline at East Penn Junction with Jersey Central FM #2402 in full regalia. The crossover in the foreground was dismantled by the end of the decade; in the photo of Reading 3649 on the previous page, the switch frogs and other accessories have been removed.

A hot eastbound with three ALCO C420's roars through East Penn Jct. on its daily journey between Buffalo and Oak Island. By 1967 the two passenger lead tracks are covered with a thick mat of weeds. The power is about to duck under the Allentown Terminal Railroad track utilized by Reading and Jersey Central trains between CNJ Allentown Yard and East Penn Junction.

The view from Allentown's CNJ station finds a twenty year old SW1 #1011 switching mail and express cars. Plainly visible are the freight station, team track and Hamilton St. watchman tower. The crossing gates lowered by a hand pump. April 1962.

Iron Horse Rambles always drew great crowds to trackside. The May 18, 1963, ramble to Elsmere Junction, Delaware, from Bethlehem and Allentown was no exception. The Allentown passengers have left the train and look around for the shortest path from Hamilton Street to their automobiles. The train will back out of the terminal to East Penn Junction before continuing to Bethlehem. Steam power was changed to diesel at Reading on the return trip.

As viewed from the Lehigh Valley Railroad right of way at East Penn Junction, train 1104 heads for Jersey City with a beautiful Fairbanks Morse Train Master at the head end. Canadian National boxcars loaded with newsprint set off for delivery to the Morning Call keep a Northern Pacific mechanical reefer company. The rising steam is from the Allentown incineration plant late in 1962. After scooting over the Lehigh Valley mainline, the train crosses the Lehigh River on the Allentown Terminal Railroad bridge to get back to CNJ rails.

A pair of sleek ALCO PA1 passenger diesels power a westbound mixed freight into East Penn Junction on the Lehigh Valley mainline on a foggy morning late in 1962. The previous year, all mainline passenger service on the Valley had been eliminated. With no more passengers to whisk between Buffalo and New York City, the stylish PA1's were assigned to freights, often in pairs.

The "World of Mirth" show lays over on the LV's West End Branch with vintage equipment. The line to the Allentown Fairgrounds was intact in September 1962.

CNJ's Allentown station, located at Hamilton and Race Streets, became a lonely place in the 1960's. The station, with its tall tower, was a landmark for decades. During its heyday, passengers could travel to Scranton, Jersey City, Philly and Harrisburg on Reading and CNJ trains. The LVRR operated from its own station a few steps west on Hamilton Street. Clearly visible are the freight station and watchman's tower on Hamilton Street. The street lamps are decorated for Christmas 1969.

Lehigh Valley's Allentown station was actually built right over Jordan Creek in 1890. This is a view looking west on Hamilton St. on April 14, 1962, shortly before the station was torn down. Photo by Stephen Drofitz.

Powered by FM Train Master 2402, Saturday-only train 1192 is ready for departure from Allentown. The New York *Clocker* will depart 12:45 PM EST and make more than a dozen stops on its trip to Jersey City Terminal on this July 1961 day. Tracks in the foreground belong to the LVRR.

With the elimination of passenger service the LVRR passenger mainline through Allentown was reduced to a single secondary track and all signals removed. A lone red and white upper quadrant semaphore erected in the ballast was a reminder of a more colorful time at Gap Junction, milepost 95. There is also a Gap Jct. on the L&NE, where their line splits to go to Palmerton.

Summer 1962 in Allentown... Hamilton Street crossing is still protected by this venerable watchman's tower; the Arbogast and Bastian powerhouse stack rises over their meat packing plant along the Lehigh River; boxcars are sitting at local warehouses and telephone call boxes are painted black with a yellow stripe. Photo taken with Ektachrome 32 film.

A westbound has stopped at Allentown. This view near the gas works storage facility shows the Automatic Train Stop on the far left track, just beyond the crossing. Two-year old number 303 was one of 4 GP18 models built during 1960.

Ironton 751 works its way west from Coplay with a train of bituminous destined for the local cement mill. The tracks on the left side of no. 751 lead to the Coplay Cement Mfg. Co. Cement loadings for the railroad were already in decline when this photo was taken in 1963.

Passenger service along the Ironton Railroad ended in 1921. The wooden combine found a new use as maintenance of way office on the mainline between Stiles and Egypt.

One of two Baldwin DS4-4-10 models purchased for the Ironton in 1949, number 751 is coupled to caboose number 8 at Hokendauqua to start work on a warm summer day in 1970. The little line was purchased from Thomas Iron Co. in 1923 jointly by Lehigh Valley and Reading. The Baldwins were built and painted to Reading Company specifications, including the inverted "V" rain gutter on the cab roof! The well maintained switcher survived long enough to be owned and operated by Conrail until 1977.

At the other end of the cement belt, the northeastern tip of Northampton County at Portland, the crew of an Erie-Lackawanna local freight walk back to their automobile for the ride home. The late afternoon sun sets on another day of railroading in the cement belt in 1968. The E-L trackage extended to Pen Argyl, Bath, and Martins Creek over ex-DLW trackage. Portland was connected to the E-L mainline at Slateford Junction. The Portland-Columbia Route 611 bridge is visible in the distance.

A pair of C628's slice though the ruins of the Thomas Iron Company at Hokendauqua. Two additional main tracks abandoned in the late 1950's have been replaced by weeds.

A view of the LVRR mainline from the Coplay to Northampton bridge in 1963. The Ironton Railroad mainline to Egypt passes directly behind the Coplay station.

Following the curving Lehigh River between Coplay and Cementon, a westbound manifest behind RS11 402 and ALCO and EMD boosters passes the site where Portland cement was first produced in the United States. The Saylor Portland Cement kilns are visible in the distance. July 1961.

SW8 Number 266 drops down a steep grade after delivering two loads of bituminous coal to Whitehall Cement during Spring 1966.

ALCO's and EMD run side by side at the Whitehall Cement Yard. The PA's are making the daily pick up of loaded covered cement hoppers.

"Snowbirds" aptly describe the brand new C628's as they fly thru Cementon with a yellowjacket C420 on a bright winter day. The 630 has just been delivered in November, and seems to be enjoying her first of twenty-one winters flying the flag for LV.

In the twilight of their freight-hauling career, two PA1 passenger units smoke it up as they accelerate west through Cementon with a Frisco boxcar and a long string of hoppers in March 1964. All but one of the PA1's would be scrapped by year's end.

As 1963 draws to a close, a pair of ALCO PA1's curl their train around Whitehall Cement's landmark silos with westbound freight on Cementon's famous superelevated curve. Photo by William C. Kulp.

Fresh snow is kicked up by a hotshot early in 1965. Reefers on the headend contains produce destined for New York City.

The incredible four track mainline through Laury's Station (Laurys in the LVRR timetable) is reduced to a single track in this early 1969 scene. Two big ALCO C628's easily handle eastbound tonnage which is dwindling fast due to the Penn Central merger. Fifty years earlier, six through and eight local passenger trains ran daily in both directions, along with dozens of freight trains.

PA1's 601 and 610 are leaving Cementon with loads bound for Richards Yard near Easton. The superior quality of the Lehigh Valley is evidenced by the heavy rail that was used for the siding into Whitehall Cement.

A midday freight races west and is about to cross PA Route 329 in Cementon. The mainline was still double track with 136 pound rail in July 1961. GP18 304 is just over a year old.

While road freights saw a variety of power, there is no doubt that the EMD "pups" were the undisputed kings of the local work. Repainted in the new simplified PRR-inspired scheme, SW8 251 holds down the Cementon Drill during Spring 1966.

The Cementon Drill gives new meaning to push-pull operations. Pushing two LVRR hoppers, a late afternoon drill pulls empty boxcars and covered hoppers en route to Cementon.

Setting out a Southern Pacific 50 foot boxcar of lumber at Kern's Lumber Yard in Slatington proves to be a challenge when the engineer is working with an A-B-B-A set of F7's. Flanges on the F's were squealing loudly as the big locomotives backed thru the S-curves into the lumber yard. Note the old-time crossbucks guarding the road crossing in Spring 1968.

Road power returns to the mainline after setting out the car.

The brakeman returns to the cab after aligning the switchpoints one to one. The secondary track belongs to the abandoned Slatedale Branch to Little Run Junction and Saegersville Quarry 4 miles west. Reading Company's Schuylkill and Lehigh "Berksy" branch terminated at Little Run Junction, but ended service in 1961. Slatington station looms in the distance.

The late 1960's found much of the LVRR mainline single-tracked. The F's begin to pull away after making the setout. The station, once used by LV, L&NE and Reading, would succumb to a major derailment on February 1, 1969... less than a year away.

Built during 1862, the year before Lincoln's Gettysburg Address, Slatington's Lehigh Valley Railroad station was one of the oldest surviving structures on the original line between Easton and Jim Thorpe. The Asa Packer Mansion was built in 1861. The station survived intact until the morning of February 1, 1969. An Oak Island to Buffalo freight derailed at track speed scattering 31 cars over a wide area. The station was severely damaged. Even the old six-inch water main once used to supply steam locomotives burst underneath the station. The remaining structure was razed after the mainline reopened.

The Pottsville Branch turned west from Lizard Creek Junction, mile 115. The turnout is now covered in weeds as an eastbound symbol freight picks up speed through the plant. The branch extended 40 miles to Blackwood. All that is left of the branch is a little-used siding.

A Central Vermont outside braced boxcar is set out on a siding at Slatington. Main Street is blocked for more than a few minutes as they perform this old fashion ritual. Friction bearing trucks as seen on the N&W boxcar would soon pass into history.

All Lehigh Valley C420's originally wore the yellowjacket paint; one quarter of the fleet is shown here, just over two years after delivery. The 408, 411 and 406 are ready to depart on the high iron with a road local to upstate New York. The large hill behind the lead unit consists of mine tailings from abandoned open pit slate quarries which dot the area around Slatington.

Derailments on the Lehigh Valley were infrequent but when they did occur they were spectacular, due to the high speed running. The wreck at Bowmanstown derailed two dozen cars in Nov. 1966. All freight was diverted to the CNJ line on the opposite bank of the Lehigh River, as illustrated by the westbound LV freight in the background led by a C420 and 2 C628's. The people at Transport Leasing, owner of covered hopper TLDX 2014 that "flipped its lid", were surely not amused by this sight.

An RS11, leased from parent PRR, idles between assignments at Lehighton early in 1967. This unit had worn number 8654 only a few weeks earlier, and was returned to the PRR by Autumn. Note the interesting variety of rolling stock present.

Lehigh Valley SW9 works the east end of Packerton Yard in March 1969. A small passenger car yard was located to the right of this area during the passenger train era.

On a cold and dreary winter day in 1965, big ALCO's with short noses and little ALCO's with long noses are inspected for defects across from the Lehighton engine house while awaiting their next assignments.

Packerton Yard was once filled with thousands of carloads of anthracite coal, but is of little use to management in 1968. The Packerton Shops in the distance employed up to 2000 men in the days of steam!

FA2 idles between assignments at Lehighton early in 1965. Within a year the 586 would be traded-in on C628 Snowbirds.

An all-Schenectady FA/FB/RS11/RS11 lashup waits in the sprawling Packerton Yard for its next assignment. Those plugs on the nose of the 582 are multiple-unit receptacles, added by ALCO after a wreck in 1959.

An Allentown to Lehighton local on the CNJ-LV connecting track holds for yarding instructions at Lehighton tower. The CNJ right of way seen to the left was abandoned in 1965.

In Lehighton, the LVRR freight house was utilized for maintenance of way storage in the 1960's. View is looking south (timetable east) at Lehighton Interlocking from the CNJ right of way.

A Lehigh Valley crewmember on an eastbound C420 waves to his westbound CNJ counterpart on an SD40 as they pass through Packerton Yard on a dreary day in Lehighton.

The LVRR leased eight ALCO RS11 locomotives from parent Pennsylvania Railroad in 1964. Number 7651 is seen at Packerton Yard in 1967, still painted in PRR Brunswick green, with 7640 in PRR Tuscan red. Hasty renumbering from 8651 to 7651 is apparent on the cab, as the unit is readied for the Penn Central merger. The 7651 returned to the PRR before the end of the year, but 7640 stayed on the LV for good.

Two weary covered wagons idle by the Lehighton engine house on a July 1967 afternoon. Within six months the 17-year old F7A 560 would be retired and sold.

54

ALCO'S TO ALLENTOWN

Lehigh Valley F7A 564 and booster idle away in the bright winter sunshine at Lehighton. The Valley owned 14 F7s, eight A units and 6 B units. Delivered by EMD in 1950 they were a part of Lehigh Valley's Cornell red covered wagon freight fleet: 8 FT's, 14 F7, 20 F3, 20 FA/FB-1, and 12 FA/FB2 models.

On a cold clear winter afternoon in 1967 there is action at Lehighton as a Buffalo to Oak Island symbol freight with an A-B-B-A set of F's is about to duck under the CNJ mainline, which is perched upon the fill. The tracks at the engine house are filled with an assortment of EMD power.

Three wooden MOW bunk cars and a cabin car are spotted behind the Lehighton freight house in Spring 1965. A blue signal lantern on the cabin protects the cars from being moved per Rule 26.

A unique set of roadswitchers back to their train at Lehighton on a clear winter day in 1968 -- GP18, original LV RS11 and a Pennsy leased RS11. Look at the bell placement on the roof of 302!!!

Westbound CNJ freight led by leased B&O SD40 and CNJ SD35 has entered Packerton Yard via the 1965 connection. The original CNJ roadbed lies abandoned overhead in March 1968.

Train symbol JC 3 rounds the last curve into Jim Thorpe (Mauch Chunk). The Lehigh Gorge deepens into a whitewater canyon with limited access by automobile.

The ground shakes as JC 3 rumbles by Jim Thorpe station. The old LV station at Mauch Chunk was situated across the river near the ACME market, visible just in front of the first unit.

There is still enough business to maintain operations at Nesquehoning Junction (PQ) in March 1968. The Nesquehoning Valley Branch terminated 16.72 miles west at Tamanend.

An A-B-B-A set of F's departs Lehighton with a mix of boxcars and hoppers. Track work is under way to complete a connection with the CNJ in 1965. The spur to the right goes to the old passenger yard.

RS11 7643 idles near SW8 264 at Packerton in 1968. Take note of the railroader looking back at 264... Lehigh Valley railroaders always dressed neatly in appropriate rugged railroad attire.

In the Summer of 1970, both the CNJ and LV are moving merchandise through the Lehigh Narrows. CNJ's Jim Thorpe station is on the near side of the river, while the old Lehigh Valley Mauch Chunk station was located to the right of the bridge, where an ACME supermarket and parking lot now stand. Asa Packer's mansion is located on the hillside beyond the CNJ station. Photographed from Flagstaff Park by Elaine W. Serensits.

Posing in front of CNJ's Jim Thorpe station is wooden caboose 31355 and RSD4 1606 during the Summer of '69. The town was served by a 14-track yard, engine house and turntable -- all west of the station.

A small yard and engine facility were maintained by the CNJ at Jim Thorpe. Sand and diesel fuel were available as seen here in August 1969. Most of the structures dated back to the steam era. Number 1554 was originally assigned to commuter service in New Jersey. One of its last assignments in Pennsylvania was to pull the "hospital train" of CNJ equipment to New Jersey on March 31, 1972. CNJ operations in Pennsylvania were terminated at that time.

A lone switcher idles away at the CNJ Jim Thorpe engine house in late summer 1969. The turntable remained operable but the engine house sat unused. Access to the site was obtained by way of the wooden steps leading down from US 209.

A rotting post-Civil War day coach once served as a yard office hard by the hillside adjacent to the Mauch Chunk engine house.

Dual FM Train Masters snake through the 6-degree S-curves at Palmerton. They pass under the Chestnut Ridge Railway and approach HX Tower controlling the east end of the yard servicing the New Jersey Zinc Company.

The ground lays covered in snow in Palmerton as JC 3 approaches HX Tower and the Palmerton Yard. The huge New Jersey Zinc works was in operation when this photo was snapped in early 1967, yet the CNJ yard is almost void of cars... an omen of lean times ahead.

Lehigh Gap hosted not only three railroads but also a cantilevered Pennsylvania Route 248. Spring is just around the corner in 1965 as a westbound CNJ freight enters the Gap.

Brand new in 1972, GP38AC number 310 and older GP9 301 head west along the CNJ's Lehigh & Susquehanna mainline at Lockport (milepost 102.5). Both locomotives show off a change in LV paint styles. The 310 was delivered with a bright Cornell red body and tall yellow LEHIGH VALLEY lettering on the long hood. The 301 sported a wide yellow band that was also applied to RS3 number 216. The photo was taken while driving north along Route 145.

Lehigh Valley and CNJ began sharing facilities in the Spring of 1965. This westbound LV freight is winding its way through Palmerton during Summer 1967 on CNJ trackage. The CNJ mainline was removed from service between Lehighton and Packerton. The CNJ line was also pulled up between Hetchel and White Haven to eliminate duplicate trackage in mountainous areas. Number 410 is a ALCO C420, one of a dozen that were placed in service during 1964. The dynamic brakes were put to good use west of Mauch Chunk.

A westbound out of Allentown is running reverse main due to a derailment at Treichler. The house on the right once served the toll collector for a chain bridge which crossed the Lehigh River here. This location is also known as Weiders Crossing. Lehigh Canal Guard Lock #3 and Dam #3 were a short distance downriver from the chain bridge.

Chestnut Ridge Railway number 10 heads west to New Jersey Zinc's Hazard Plant at Palmerton. The porch steps of the aging ALCO S2 (blt 1946) provide a cool ride through the hot and humid air of July 1967. The tracks below belong to the CNJ.

A derailment immediately west of Treichler station has blocked CNJ mainline. This westbound Lehigh Valley freight will spend an afternoon waiting for one track to be cleared. The switch is for Mauser Milling at mile 100.

Treichler as seen from Pa. Highway 145 after the wreck. An eastbound LVRR freight heads to Allentown Yard. A damaged Western Maryland hopper has been spotted near the depot. The Bethlehem tool cars are spotted on the center siding. The wreck crane is working on the westbound track behind the photographer.

A sandwich of first and second generation EMD's work west at Treichler, milepost 100. The CNJ leased the Baltimore & Ohio F7A's to help alleviate a power shortage in 1968; the railroad's mechanical department was overwhelmed with broken down motive power. The switch in the foreground leads to the center siding between Treichler and Lockport -- a distance of two and one half miles.

Venerable F3 number 516 heads an all-EMD lash up westbound over CNJ rails at Treichler in late Spring 1966. The F3 rated 1500HP when built by EMD in 1948.

FM Train Master 2406 blows through Treichler on a cold and clear day in Winter 1967. The old brown paint may be peeling on the depot, but Mauser Milling is busy next door.

Headed for Wilkes-Barre, AC 3 works west past the Pennsylvania Power & Light substation north of Northampton, powered by an SD35 and a RS3 in the last days of Summer in 1967. Wanko's greenhouse is nearby... a favorite place for locals to purchase flowers, vegetable plants and pumpkins in the Fall.

A lone semaphore drops to stop position as CA 6 from Taylor Yard barrels toward Siegfried station with a pair of RSD's in 1965. The Pennsylvania German stone farm house and out buildings are a familiar sight in the historic Lehigh River Valley.

At Treichler, a light rain is falling on a steamy July 1967 day as a CNJ track inspector in a rain slicker examines the latest in a number of derailments plaguing the near-bankrupt line. The Allentown wreck train has been called.

Reading Number 541 (Baldwin AS-16) provides mobility to CNJ wreck crane number 5. The BAR "State of Maine" potato car has been shoved off the right of way as progress is made on clearing the eastbound track.

Steam powered number 5 pulls the hopper toward the crane. It will then be righted and set on replacement trucks. One by one the cars are emptied, righted and set on shop trucks. Track crews laid replacement rails on new ties as space allowed. Note workmen placing heavy blocking under the crane. The gearing visible on the left side operated like the mechanism of a Swiss watch.

With the super looking on, workmen toil to clear up the derailment. The American diesel crane is emptying each damaged hopper to expedite clean up operations.

Weeds are a constant problem, and Reade Mfg. Co. provided relief with a heavy application of vegetation killer. This spray train is working in the Allen Cement Branch yard during the Summer of 1961. This yard serviced the Allen Cement Company, later known as the Dragon Cement Company, a subsidiary of Martin Marietta.

As part of CNJ's summer trackwork in 1965, ballast from CNJ hoppers is deposited on the westbound main near mile 96, west of Siegfried. Note crewmember standing in car.

Prior to rigid environmental laws it was possible to find CNJ knocking down weeds with this unique flame thrower. The operator is tidying up track at the Northampton and Bath interchange under the Coplay (9th Street) bridge in Northampton in 1969.

An SD35, RS3 and two RSD's whip up the dust as they roar west past Siegfried in September, 1965. The station still stands today, but the freight house is long gone. Notice the cloud of smoke erupting from the stacks of the three aging ALCO's that is beginning to drift over the Lehigh River.

The CNJ was not a heavily ballasted line. As a matter of fact, much of the mainline was ballasted with slag, easily accessible from the various slag dumps in the Lehigh River valley. The slag dumps are a reminder of the seventeen iron furnaces that dotted the area in the late 19th century. The ALCO RSD4's are hurrying a ballast train west and have just cleared the 17th Street crossing in Northampton in October 1965. The middle track is the local track for the shifter.

SW1 1011 heads west towards Siegfried station and the Dragon Cement Company in 1966. The view is from the shifter servicing Northampton Yard and the Atlas Cement Company cars. Our location is directly underneath the Northampton to Coplay bridge. The track veering off to the right was a spindly trestle built in 1884 that the CNJ built to interchange with the Ironton Railroad in Coplay.

A wood caboose brings up the rear of the Allentown to Siegfried local. This drill will switch cars at the Dragon Cement Company on the other end of town.

One of the few buildings left standing from Atlas Cement Co.'s plant 2, 3, and 4 at Northampton was the huge machine shop. With construction of plant 5 in 1941, the Northampton & Bath RR was able to abandon a nearby structure in favor of the surplus machine shop. Locomotive and freight car repair were carried on here. Most of the line was abandoned in 1978, and the rest in 1984. The remaining trackage is now operated by NDC.

Bought from L&NE, cabooses 102 and 103 were of composite construction. N&B shop crews removed the cupola from each caboose in 1966. They are shown here shortly after their conversion and repainting.

Brand new SD35's 2509 and 2510 and a lone RSD head north (timetable west). The giant lot provided free parking for patrons of Newberry's, Miller's, Coleman's, The Roxy Theatre, Northampton Home Furnishers, Lerners and other establishments in Northampton's Main Street business district. This is the former site of Miller's field, where the Northampton Buffaloes played baseball and the Northampton Triangles played football. I did my tree climbing in late Spring 1965.

This overhead view of a cement local approaching Siegfried station (the station and the separate freight house are clearly visible) shows the west end of Northampton's middle siding with the Dragon Cement Company towering in the distance. An old coal trestle lies to the left of the mainline in the foreground. Many towns in the Lehigh Valley had coal trestles to service the Anthracite home heating business. In the grassy field to the right stands the monument to Colonel John Siegfried.

Two views of Northampton station. The borough was privileged to have two stations along the Jersey Central -- Northampton and Siegfried. The villages of Stemton, Newport, and Siegfried incorporated as Alliance on May 6, 1901. The name was officially changed to Northampton on April 12, 1909. There could be confusion with two stations of the same name. By timetable the east station was named Northampton, and the west station remained Siegfried. The near track in the top photo is a siding into the Tru Blu Brewery (closed in 1951). Many years ago, boxcars filled with bushel baskets of grapes were brought in during fall for the local residents to purchase in order to make wine!

A motive power mix heads west at Northampton. It was somewhat uncommon to see ALCO roadswitchers leading EMD's on westbounds. The siding against the embankment leads to the team track behind the freight station at Siegfried.

Snow blankets the borough of Northampton as westbound JC 3 approaches 21st Street. An old coal yard trestle survives without track along Canal Street in December 1961.

The crossing gates are down at 21st Street, and the engineer is sounding the air horns on his F3 as he labors west through Northampton with AC 3. This photo was on my first roll of Kodachrome ASA10 photographed with a Kodak Pony IV on a hot day in Summer, 1961.

The days are growing short and the light is fading fast on this cold day late in 1962 as AC 3 rambles west with a mile long mixed freight.

A Sunday morning fog is lifting over Northampton as a long freight rumbles east through town. The TOFC traffic added a new dimension to CNJ freight consists. The marker lamps appear to be of the kerosene type and still in use in May 1965.

Three small critters in the Pennsylvania cement belt: A diminutive industrial switcher shoves an L&NE boxcar to a loading dock at the Dragon Cement Co. on the north side of Northampton in 1965.

A Dragon Cement Co. industrial switcher and two loaded hoppers of lime-stone from quarry number two return to the cement mill for further processing during the Summer of '67.

Safety orange industrial switcher from National Portland Cement Co. of Bethlehem, Pa., is spotted outside the N&B Railroad shop in Northampton in 1968. The diesel shop originally served as a machine shop for the Atlas Cement Plant which was built around this site in 1895.

Allentown to Scranton train AC 3 is making a pickup at the lower end of town in Northampton Yard.

Northampton & Bath caboose number 102 was purchased from the L&NE. This is the same caboose pictured on page 74 before undergoing its conversion.

Wooden snowplow 353 was sold to the CNJ after the L&NE Railroad abandonment. The snowplow was stored serviceable at Tadmor in 1966. In this view, the plow sports its headlight, while the photo on page 82 shows the plow without its headlight.

Lehigh & New England caboose 583 was one of five all steel USRA design built by Reading Company in 1937. It is not known whether Mr. Magoo was a stowaway, railfan or L&NE employee.

BLH AS-16's and ALCO RSD4 share former L&NE Tadmor terminal on a cold winter day in 1968. CNJ picked up cement belt trackage and facilities from Lehigh & New England after the line sold their operations in 1961.

A striped RSD4 works Tadmor yard on a warm summer day in 1967 while a weary crewmember takes a short break. Look at those switchlamps!!!

Equipment normally assigned to Tadmor was reassigned to an improvised facility near CNJ's Bethlehem station. Note that the headlight is not attached to the plow in this view (see page 81) taken during Summer 1970. The 1615 is the only RSD5 in CNJ's diesel fleet.

CNJ owned 10 "Babyface" Baldwin DR4-4-15 cab units and 5 boosters. They had 8-cylinder prime movers rated at 1500HP that produced a deep throaty thumping sound under load. DR4-4-15's produced after 1949 were of the sharknose carbody design. The Baldwins could not be mu'd with locomotives from another manufacturer; a booster or cab unit down for service could mean two units down. No. 77 is waiting for its booster (B unit) to complete servicing at the Bethlehem Engine Terminal late in 1966.

Reading GP7 633 sports a new bright yellow and green paint scheme, first seen on the GP30's in 1962. Reading had quite an interesting assortment of information on the frame, including a safety message, the oval builders plate, an owner plate, a "1" (front) and a "2" denoting the ends of the unit -- plus the standard "F", the horsepower (1500), and Reading's locomotive class... in this case, an RS-3!!! Photographed November 5, 1966.

A water tank from a previous era looms behind the Bethelehem Engine Terminal. Reading Company owned ten 2400hp C424 ALCO's.

Baldwin AS-16 #516 idles near CNJ's Bethlehem engine house. Built in 1927, the Bethlehem roundhouse / engine house complex employed more than 100 workers.

Lehigh Valley RS11 7643 spotted on one of 42 spurs of the Bethlehem Roundhouse. The 7643 is painted in one of the popular later styles with a yellow band around the entire unit and a black diamond on each end. The full striping treatment was applied to the front of the units; in the case of the 7643, it is the end with the long hood. This scheme, with variations, was applied to many of the ALCO's during the last decade of the Lehigh Valley. It was seen on C628's, C420's and hi- and lo-nose versions of the RS11.

Lehigh Valley SW900m (trade-in/heavy rebuilding from an NW1) takes a spin on the Bethlehem turntable. When this photo was taken in 1973 the CNJ presence had completely vanished.

Two Lehigh & Hudson River RS3's at the Bethlehem Engine Terminal's turntable early in 1967, await a crew for their return trip to Maybrook, New York. L&HR would acquire nine C420's to replace their aging RS3's; the last L&HR RS3 left the property in 1970. Note Reading 614 off to the left, sitting in front of one of the roundhouse doors.

Steam vapor swirls around GP7 number 1524 at the Bethlehem Engine Terminal. This dual-purpose freight and passenger loco-motive is used to power Allentown to Jersey City passenger trains. The massive coaling tower in the background was later used to sand diesels! Photo taken Winter 1967.

Two C630's with Tri-Mounts (later Reading C630's rode on Hi-Ad trucks -- see RDG 5311 on page 95), a C424 and a GP35 inch forward with a Reading manifest leaving Allentown. Trains headed to Reading were faced with a stiff 0.9% grade starting at R Tower (inside the yard) and not slacking off until they crossed above the Lehigh Valley mainline and reached East Penn Jct.

Two of the most recognizable faces in diesel lore, the Baldwin Babyface and General Motors GP30, are caught in a pose near the Bethlehem roundhouse. The Baldwins emitted a very unique sound at idle and when working on the road gave you the impression a large ocean freighter was passing nearby. The Baldwin model 608SC turbo 8-cylinder (1500hp @625rpm) was based on the De La Vergne marine engine!

The bright yellow and green Reading Company paint scheme was a welcome sight to northeast railfans. CNJ ALCO RSD4 and Reading GP35 3623 await duty at Bethlehem during summer 1967.

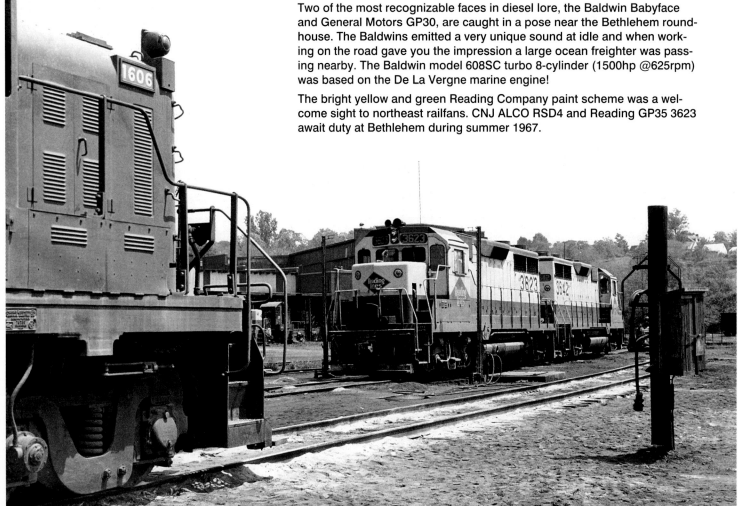

A trio of Lehigh & Hudson River ALCO C420's arrive at Allentown Yard with New England freight on a warm afternoon day in July 1967. The L&HR was an important bridge line linking New England and the Middle Atlantic States via Maybrook, New York. New Haven trains reached Maybrook via their spectacular bridge (built 1888) over the Hudson River at Poughkeepsie, New York. A fire on the bridge decking in 1974 was reason enough for Penn Central to shut down the Maybrook line and the loss of bridge traffic devastated L&HR. Number 26 was sold in 1975 to British Columbia Railway.

An old kerosene switch lantern stands vigil in Allentown Yard while the crew of RDG GP35 number 3640 chat.

Some crewmembers of LV number 140 are chatting near the westbound Allentown hump late in 1973. Their Baldwin DS4-4-1000, already a veteran performer of more than 20 years, stands ready for work in the big yard with cabooses from LV and Reading. Shoving on the hump are three LV RS11's from PRR.

Two ALCO road switchers head back to their train deep inside Allentown Yard in 1968. Beginning in 1965, CNJ and LV shared the yard, per their agreement to eliminate duplicate facilities in Pennsylvania. Number 218 is one of two ex-Chesapeake & Ohio RS2's purchased from ALCO.

Brawny ALCO C630 class unit number 5300 with Tri-Mount trucks was delivered in 1966. Its nameplate appears to read "Rocket II". The C630 and C424 5208 are awaiting clearance to depart Allentown Yard. Note the CNJ trailer sporting a Railway Express Agency mudflap on the adjacent track!

A trio of Lehigh & Hudson River ALCO C420's arrive at the Allentown hump. Unlike all the 420's on the LV, none of the L&HR C420's had dynamic brakes. It is June 1966 and the L&HR is exercising trackage rights over CNJ from Easton to access Allentown.

When the CNJ packed up and left Pennsylvania in 1972, the Lehigh Valley stepped in and took over. Replacing CNJ 5, the Allentown big hook, is LV 96534, stationed near the west end of Allentown Yard.

CNJ's Allentown tool cars accompanying their big hook number 5 make for interesting study of early freight car construction.

CNJ's answer to weed control before anyone heard of the EPA is hard at work in Allentown Yard. The burner was followed by a crew carrying water to extinguish hot spots.

The Bethlehem Engine Terminal was always an interesting place; in addition to the parade of diesels in and out of the facility, there were also interesting structures and equipment to photograph. The hulk of a 50 year old wooden CNJ caboose sitting at Bethlehem Terminal leaves little evidence of its heritage.

A CNJ RSD4 works the eastbound (heavy side) hump in the Allentown yard in Spring 1968. Both cars in the foreground are running on friction bearings. Railroading was headed for major changes, some political and some mechanical.

RSD4 #1613 prepares to cut off from road units 5207 and 3604. The old ALCO was used to help the eastbound train that stalled while entering Allentown yard. A unique set of two-bay friction bearing CNJ, RDG and B&O coal hoppers are in the foreground.

Three diesels and 3 builders... an EMD-FM-ALCO lashup (GP7/H24-16/RS3) is ready to depart for Lurgan with per diem freight AL-3. By getting empties back to the Western Maryland by midnight, Reading did not have to pay daily charges for those cars.

C630 5311 and C424 5204 ready for departure from Allentown. The switching crew on the caboose have spotted the the photographer and pose for a picture. Number 627 is a GP7 equipped with dynamic brake. The Bee Line Service (note how the Reading diamond is used for the body of the bee!) C630 was equipped with ALCO's Hi-Ad trucks.

One of six ALCO RS1 locomotives on the CNJ, number 1200 is seen working the Allentown Yard in May 1964. All six RS1's were assigned to the Southern Division in NJ, mainly pulling loads of sand. They were rarely seen in this area. A 6-cylinder model 539 Macintosh Seymour engine provided 1000HP.

A midday CNJ freight is ready for departure from Allentown. The CNJ would leave Pennsylvania entirely in 1972, with the Lehigh Valley taking over operations.

Crossing the Lehigh River at Bethlehem Junction, Bee Line U30C 6302 and C424 5205 hold down the CNJ mainline to Allentown with coal hoppers in July 1967.

One third of L&HR's fleet of ALCO Century 420's pass Bethlehem Junction on their way to Allentown Yard. Heavy eastbound traffic would require light engine and caboose moves to Allentown from Warwick.

Eastbound freight passes abandoned JU tower at Bethlehem Junction. By 1967, CNJ's fleet of aging road power reached a critical mass. The Elizabethport shops were overwhelmed with units requiring repair. An immediate infusion of leased N&W and B&O F7's went to work along with a dozen SD35 locomotives purchased new in 1966 from EMD.

The constant drone of Mauser Milling is broken by the chant of EMD 567 prime movers. Lead F3A number 514 was turned out by EMD in 1948. July 1967

The engineer is sounding the horns on the striped F3 as he races thru Northampton on a Spring day in 1963 with AC 3. The hoggers really opened up the throttle when they rounded the curve below 9th Street. By the time they reached 21st Street they were really flying!

Train watching opportunities during this period were incredible. However, the intensity of railfanning as we know it today did not exist. The late '50's and early '60's can only be described as a transition period. Steam power was banished from the mainlines of America and diesels were firmly established as the motive power of choice. An entire generation of train watchers were saddened by the demise of steam. Many put down their cameras and abandoned their favorite pastime, never to return trackside. Others failed to capture on film the changeover to diesel. If there was a choice between capturing a shiny new F3 or a retired and capped steam locomotive, the latter was chosen. There was a true passion involved here. For us in the baby boom generation, there was no choice...we only knew about the shiny new diesels. My early memories of train watching began close to home in Northampton, Pennsylvania. Growing up near two busy mainlines can easily stir the imagination of a young railfan. The Jersey Central mainline split our little town with a long tangent of north to south trackage. The town of Northampton lay on the east side of the Lehigh River along with the abandoned Lehigh Canal. The train I saw the most was the afternoon Jersey Central AC 3. This Allentown to Scranton freight train was often powered with an F3A/B set leading RSD ALCO road switchers. The locomotives would work hard through town as they picked up speed out of Allentown and Catasauqua. The Dragon Cement Co. drill from Allentown would usually take the middle passing siding to allow AC 3 to pass on the main; the siding would allow local switchers to access both yards without fouling the main tracks. After AC 3 passed, the drill would return to the westbound main and head to the Dragon Cement Co. yard on the north end of town.

The Dragon Cement Company operated two industrial switchers on their own property. These switchers moved coal hoppers and covered cement hoppers to and from the various loading and unloading areas of the huge complex. They also operated a two-car hopper train to the limestone rock crusher plant located on the edge of quarry number 2, one half mile from the main plant.

At the south end of town was a yard serving the Universal Atlas Cement Company. Here the CNJ interchanged traffic with the Northampton and Bath Railroad. Motive power was two EMD switchers. On a few occasions I had an opportunity to ride along with the switching crews as they went about their work; they were always very friendly.

The F3's and ALCO RSD's provided much of the mainline action through Northampton. Occasionally, FM Train Masters would be used. This would occur on weekends when the big FM's would not be required for passenger service in New Jersey. Two Train Masters were capable of handling AC 3.

It was very easy to detect a westbound train approaching Northampton by the sound of locomotives in run 8. Eastbound trains coming down the river valley were almost silent and would only be noticeable once the air horns blared for 21st Street crossing. One eastbound train I still remember by the sound of its prime mover... I recall a very low thumping sound in the air. It was similar to the sound of a large diesel powered laker or ocean going vessel. It turned out to be a Baldwin Babyface (DR4-4-15) headed east with a coal train. Years later I discovered the source of that incredible sound was the design of Baldwin's engine. The prime mover was based on the De La Vergne marine engine!

In 1965 CNJ received 12 new SD35 locomotives to replace the aging F3's. They were very large and more powerful than the tired F3's; however, the ALCO RSD's continued to assist the single SD35 which would often be assigned to the point of trains passing through Northampton.

A short ride on my bicycle would take me across the Lehigh River to Cementon and the Lehigh Valley Railroad mainline. A small industrial freight yard on the LVRR served the Whitehall Cement Company. The Cementon drill working out of South Easton switched the yard. The crews were very friendly and I had more than a few rides with them and their SW8. Cementon also provided for some big time railroad thrills. The LVRR mainline was very impressive,

Two of the nicest men I knew on the Lehigh Valley... Mr. Grube, the engineer, and Mr. Gallagher, the fireman, pose in the cab of SW8 number 266 at Cementon in May 1962.

more so than the CNJ running through Northampton. Laid with heavy rail on a generous bed of ballast, the LVRR timetable allowed passenger and freight trains FFW-1, FFW-3 and BJ-2, speeds of up to 60 mph between Buffalo and New York City. Lower class freight trains were allowed 50 mph.

At mid-decade, big ALCO locomotives were purchased by the Lehigh Valley Railroad. The ALCO C420's would often be used on hot trains between Oak Island and Buffalo. I chased one of the FFW-1's on a summer evening in the mid 1960's from Cementon to Lehighton. The timetable distance between Cementon and Lehighton is exactly 19 miles. The FFW-1 was scheduled to leave Oak Island, New Jersey, at 7:45pm and arrive 452 miles away at Buffalo (Tifft Terminal) at 7:45am the following morning. On that memorable night the engineer of FFW-1 sounded his horn for the Cementon crossing sometime after 10pm. I was on the wrong side of the crossing at Cementon and lost valuable time waiting for traffic to clear the gates before starting my adventure. I headed northwest along the LVRR mainline. The FFW-1 had three new powerful ALCO C420's in yellow and grey and was way ahead of me. I caught

up with his caboose at the Lehigh River bridge at Treichler. At this point the main highway crosses to the east bank of the Lehigh River. The LVRR hugs the west bank and is at least one mile distant from the highway and out of view for a long way. Finally at Lehigh Gap I drew along side FFW-1. The engineer was not slacking on his speed of 50 to 60 mph. I personally remember maintaining more than 60 mph when the road was clear! From Lehigh Gap to Lehighton the highway broadened to four lanes and I was able to pace the train to the Lehigh River bridge at Weissport. I will always remember the sight of the FFW-1 racing along the Lehigh River that moonlit night so long ago. At this point I turned around and headed home with a cherished memory of that night run to Lehighton.

Lehighton itself was an excellent train watching town. The Lehigh Valley Railroad maintained a large marshaling yard, Packerton car shops, interlocking tower and roundhouse. It was very easy to watch and photograph trains. CNJ trains began using the LVRR mainline from Lehighton Interlocking to Jim Thorpe in 1965. The CNJ trackage skirting the LVRR yard was abandoned. Traveling deeper into the Lehigh

Gorge would bring you to Jim Thorpe. The CNJ maintained a beautiful station downtown. They also operated a small yard and engine house with turntable west (by timetable) of the station. The view of both CNJ and LVRR from the station platform was spectacular! Not to be missed was the Asa Packer Mansion overlooking downtown Jim Thorpe. Asa Packer (1805-1879) was instrumental in the creation of the Lehigh Valley Railroad and remained in control of the railroad until his death.

Other major train watching locations on the LV were West Catasauqua, East Penn Junction, Allentown Yard and Bethlehem Roundhouse. West Catasauqua was a major interchange at one time for Reading Company, Lehigh Valley, Lehigh & New England and Ironton Railroads. By the mid 1960's the bottom had fallen out of the railroad cement hauling business and things changed. Much of the Lehigh & New England was abandoned. The Reading Company closed their yard at West Catasauqua, leaving the Lehigh Valley Railroad's Biery Yard to handle the remaining cement business. The Ironton Railroad

managed to remain busy through the end of the decade working with the Lehigh Valley Railroad connection at Biery Yard. A number of through and local trains could be seen and photographed at West Catasauqua.

East Penn Junction in Allentown was a very interesting place to watch trains. The wye funneled Reading Company freight trains into Allentown Yard. It also allowed passenger trains to enter Allentown CNJ station from the Reading Company Harrisburg line and CNJ's New York line. Passing under the east leg of the wye was the Lehigh Valley mainline. This, too, was connected to the south side of the wye by multiple tracks curving back to the Reading Company line. The Lehigh Valley Railroad would drop off boxcar loads of Canadian newsprint for Allentown newspapers at this junction. I often visited with the watchman in his elevated tower located in the center of East Penn Junction. He was responsible for the crossing gates on Basin Street. The crossing gates were operated by a hand pump with power provided by the watchman; it was a very physically demanding job.

A once-common Northeastern-style LV steel caboose is coupled to a pup in preparation for drilling Whitehall Cement's yard.

East Penn Junction was an impressive place to view railroad action in July 1961. Train Master 867 rumbles past the watchman's tower and under the signal bridge en route to Allentown Yard. Tracks descended to the left to a connection with LVRR. Tracks leading to the Allentown CNJ passenger station and beyond to Scranton are on the right. The crossing gates were lowered and raised by the strength and power of the watchman.

Reading Company's Catasauqua freight station was relocated to a site about 1000 feet west of the Lehigh Valley mainline. Originally constructed near the Lehigh Valley Railroad and Lehigh and New England crossing the entire building was moved beyond Water Street in the 1940's. The station sat empty when photographed in 1963. The station now resides on the WK&S.

Looking west from Water Street, Reading Company's Catasauqua yard is devoid of freight cars in 1963.

Action at East Penn Junction was intense, with seemingly nonstop passenger and freight action in the early 1960's.

Allentown Yard was the pivotal point to watch trains arriving or departing the city. River Road from East Allentown to Bethlehem parallels the north side of the yard. An overlook near the westbound hump offered a grand view of the entire yard. Bethlehem Engine Terminal was usually a friendly place, and weekend mornings would find a few "fans" on tour near the turntable and old coaling tower. The engine house tracks and fuel/sand facility were always loaded with locomotives from Reading and Jersey Central, and later, Lehigh Valley.

Other areas to watch mainline railroading in the Lehigh Valley were Bethlehem Union Station, Saucon Yard and Easton. The Bethlehem Union station was near the CNJ-LV connection crossing the Lehigh River on a realigned span. Lehigh Valley Railroad trains entered Allentown Yard or headed west on the their old mainline from this point. The Reading Company continued to run Philadelphia passenger trains from Union Station after the LVRR abandoned its passenger service.

Easton provided some spectacular bridge photography with three major spans belonging to the LVRR, L&HR and CNJ. A visit to LV's South Easton shop would always prove interesting. Numerous switching drills originated daily from South Easton and many locomotive types could be seen at the engine house.

The Pennsy, and later Penn Central, maintained a locomotive servicing facility at Phillipsburg, just south of the Lehigh Valley mainline. A turntable, coaling dock and other steam-era structures remained intact into the 1960's at Phillipsburg.

Lesser known areas to visit in the 1960's were places like Portland, Nazareth and Tadmor -- all in Northampton County. Portland, in the very northeast part of the county, sported a tiny Erie-Lackawanna yard which was connected to their mainline at Slateford Jct. The E-L maintained trackage into the cement belt towns of Pen Argyl, Nazareth and Bath. The CNJ acquired Tadmor Yard and cement belt trackage by way of the L&NE abandonment.

With so many interesting places to visit, the obvious happened; many locations and operations were never or rarely photographed.

During the decade of the 1960's, ALCO locomotives were in abundance on road freights throughout the Lehigh River Valley. The Lehigh Valley Railroad quickly dieselized its road fleet between the end of World War II and the Korean War. First came 8 EMD FT's, then 20 EMD F3's, and 14 F7's. From ALCO came 20 FA/B-1's and 12 FA/B-2's. ALCO handled the mainline passenger fleet with 14 PA1's -- despite substantial passenger service, the LV never owned an EMD E-unit. By 1960 this mix of road power would gradually change to second generation. The FT's vanished first, followed by the FA/B's. They were replaced with 2 GP9's in 1959 and 4 GP18's in 1960. Four RS11's arrived in 1960 with chop noses. Twelve grey and yellow C420's arrived in 1964. They bought 8 new C628's starting in 1965 and 9 slightly used Monon C628's in 1967. The big Century models allowed the Lehigh Valley to begin retiring the F3's and F7's. The road also leased 8 RS11's from parent Pennsy in 1964, returning two in 1967. This would

end the purchase of new power until 1971-1972 when 4 GP38AC and 12 GP38-2 locomotives were purchased from EMD. The last new power was financed by the United States Railroad Administration; twelve General Electric U23B models were purchased in 1974. What all this meant is that on the mainline in 1960 you could see trains pulled by solid A-B-B-A sets of ALCO FA/B's or EMD F's. You could also see a mix of GP9 or GP18 roadswitchers leading an A-B set of EMD F's. ALCO FA/B locomotives might be coupled to a pair of RS11's. Different locomotives models were routinely mated together.

Although you could find almost any type of LV power anywhere, the pusher assignments in the 70's often fell to the C628's. The big six-axle 200-ton C628's were riding on old style Tri-Mount trucks which produced excessive wheel flange and rail wear. Many of their final miles for the Valley would be accumulated working low speed drag and helper service east of Sayre.

A look at the cab interior of a Lehigh Valley ALCO roadswitcher at Treichler.

Leased PRR RS11 8640 will be renumbered to 7640 for the Penn Central merger. This LVRR train is running on CNJ iron just west of Siegfried station in Northampton, Pa. The building with the round roof is part of Cross Country Clothes, who manufactured millions of navy blue and khaki slacks during World War II. The factory encompasses 140,000 square feet.

Train Master 867 was the first of two H24-66's repainted bright yellow and green. Seen here in Allentown in July 1967, the Beloit-produced H24-66 was the ultimate locomotive from Fairbanks Morse when constructed in 1955. The 12 cylinders and 24 opposed pistons cranked out 2400HP and 97,100 pounds of tractive effort. The unit weighed in at almost 200 tons -- 388,400 lbs.

The front, or business, end of Reading Train Master 867. Note the placement of the horn into the carbody!

The Lehigh and Hudson River replaced their fleet of 13 ALCO RS3's with 9 striking blue and grey C420's between 1963 and 1966. Usual practice found a trio of these Centuries hauling freight between Allentown and Maybrook. The units would layover between assignments at the Bethlehem Engine Terminal.

The Central Railroad of New Jersey relied heavily on their ALCO fleet. On the Allentown to Scranton run, usual power was a F3A/B with two or three RS3's or RSD4's. This combination of EMD leading ALCO was standard fare during the 1960's. Fairbanks Morse Train Masters and Babyface Baldwins were rarely seen west of Allentown. The CNJ stabled 6 RS1's, 19 RS3's, 14 RSD4's, and 1 RSD5. The RS1's were assigned to southern New Jersey, but number 1200 was seen in Allentown on at least one occasion. Mid-decade the CNJ purchased 12 SD35's and leased 9 Baltimore & Ohio SD40's. The usual lashup was an SD35 leading two or three ALCO RS's or RSD's west of Allentown. In the late '60's, 20 F7's were leased, ten each from Norfolk & Western and B&O. Again, the F7's were mixed with ALCO's and SD35's.

The Reading Company also maintained a fleet of power from different manufacturers. In the early 1960's they were powering their Reading to Allentown trains with a combination of EMD F3's, Train Masters and even Baldwin Lima-Hamilton AS-16's and ALCO FA/B's. Twenty GP30's arrived in 1962 with a new green and bright yellow paint scheme. More new power arrived to replace the aging fleet of RS3's. There were 37 GP35's by 1965. The ALCO Centuries began to arrive in 1963 -- Reading received 10 C424's. Two C430's and 7 C630's arrived in 1966, and 5 more C630's in 1967. In 1967, 5 GE U30C's and 5 EMD SD45's rounded out the fleet. Reading would not shop for power again until 1973 when they picked up 5 EMD GP40-2's. The last mainline power purchased were 20 EMD GP39-2's in 1974. The Reading Dash-2's were painted entirely in green with yellow stripes on the ends. Much of the new power was either mixed or matched on runs out of Allentown. The addition of new motive power doomed all of the first generation freight power with the exception of 44 GP7's purchased by Reading in the late 1950's.

Although most area locomotive purchases in the 1960's were big road power, some of the railroading took place on a much smaller scale, like that conducted at Lone Star Cement in Nazareth, who got along just fine with small industrial power.

EASTBOUND

Reading Co. TT #15 Eff. 2.01 A.M. EST, Sunday October 29, 1961

		AD-4	2ND HP-4	ALPHA JET-12	ALPHA JET-2	HN-5	CSD-94/HJ-4	AP 346	HCA-2	HA-2	1ST HP-4	HB-4	CSD-96/HO-6
		DAILY	DAILY	XSUN	DAILY	DAILY	DAILY	DAILY	XSUN	DAILY	DAILY	DAILY	DAILY
		A.M.	P.M.	A.M.	P.M.	P.M.	P.M.	P.M.	P.M.	P.M.	P.M.	A.M.	P.M.
LURGAN	LV			12.50	2.00		4.00						10.35
RUTHERFORD	AR	VIA		2.05	3.45		5.40						11.55
	LV	Reading	10.15	2.50		6.30	9.00		4.45	5.35	7.45	3.00	12.45
ALLENTOWN	AR						1.00			10.40		8.00	3.05
	LV	1.00											
EAST PENN JCT.	LV							1.45					
CATASAUQUA	AR									10.00			
BIRDSBORO	AR	3.15	1.30	4.25				3.15			10.10		
		A.M.	A.M.	A.M.	P.M.	P.M.	P.M.	P.M.	P.M.	P.M.	P.M.	A.M.	A.M.

LVRR TT #8 Eff. 2:01 A.M. EST, Sunday October 28, 1962

		BP-2	BM-2	SJ-2	FO-2	MC-2	BJ-2	SNE-2	BNE-2	FO-4
		DAILY	DAILY	DAILY	DAILY	DAILY	DAILY	DAILY	DAILY	DAILY
		A.M.	A.M.	A.M.	A.M.	P.M.	P.M.	P.M.	P.M.	P.M.
SUSP. BRIDGE	LV			7.30			6.00			
BUFFALO TIFFT	LV	2.00	7.30				2.05		7.30	
MANCHESTER	AR	5.00	10.00	10.30			4.45	8.45	9.45	
	LV	8.00		12.30	2.00		5.30		11.30	
SAYRE	AR	11.00		3.10		7.00	7.20		1.45	
	LV	11.45		3.55	10.15		8.00		2.30	11.00
OWEGO	AR				10.50					11.40
COXTON	AR	2.00		5.55			9.30		4.30	
	LV	2.45		6.35			9.50		5.30	
PACKERTON	AR	6.15		9.05			12.01		8.00	
	LV	7.30		10.00			12.20		8.30	
EAST PENN JCT		9.00		11.00						
BETHLEHEM		10.00								
RICHARDS		11.00					2.00		9.45	
OAK ISLAND	AR			2.00			3.30		12.01	
		P.M.	A.M.	A.M.	A.M.	P.M.	A.M.	P.M.	P.M.	P.M.

C.R.R. of N.J. TT #18 Eff. 2.01 A.M. EST, Sunday October 29, 1961

	HJ 4	HO 6	AJ 2	AY 2	AO 4	CJ 2	CA 2	FA 2	NJ 4	UJ 2	CJ 4	CA 6
	DAILY	DAILY	DAILY	EX. SU.	DAILY	DAILY	DAILY	DAILY	DAILY	DAILY	DAILY	DAILY
	A.M.	A.M.	A.M.	A.M.	A.M.	A.M.	P.M.	P.M.	P.M.	P.M.	P.M.	A.M.
SCRANTON												
TAYLOR						10.15	4.05				6.00	12.50
WILKES-BARRE						11.35	5.30				7.15	2.05
ASHLEY						11.50	5.45	3.00			7.30	3.15
PENOBSCOT						2.35		4.15				4.30
HAUCKS								10.00				
NESQ. JCT.						4.05		11.00		10.40		
JIM THORPE							8.30	6.30		9.15	4.05	6.20
WK												
R							9.35	7.45				7.30
STEEL	2.00	5.15	6.45	7.00	9.45					11.25	6.35	
BETH. JCT												
PHILLIPSBURG	2.40	5.55	7.25	7.45	10.30					12.01	7.05	
	A.M.	A.M.	A.M.	A.M.	A.M.	P.M.	P.M.	P.M.	P.M.	A.M.	A.M.	A.M.

ALCO'S TO ALLENTOWN

WESTBOUND

READING CO. #15		CAH-5	PH-3	CSD-97	PA-1	HNW-51	AL-3	TIME SAVER	DA-3	ALPHA JET-1	ADV. PH-3
EFF 2.01 10/29/61		DAILY	DAILY	DAILY	DAILY	DAILY	DAILY	XSUMO	DAILY	XSUN	DAILY
		A.M.	A.M.	A.M.	A.M.	A.M.	P.M.	P.M.	P.M.	P.M.	P.M.
BIRDSBORO	LV		2.15		10.45				9.15	10.05	11.30
ALLENTOWN	AR				12.45				11.10		
	LV			3.00			4.00	6.30			
CATASAUQUA	LV	1.00									
READING		3.00									
RUTHERFORD	AR	5.25	5.45	5.05			7.30	9.00		12.05	2.30
	LV			6.05		11.00	8.30	10.00		12.45	
LURGAN	AR			7.35		2.00	10.15	11.40		2.05	
		A.M.	A.M.	A.M.	P.M.	P.M.	P.M.	P.M.	P.M.	A.M.	A.M.

LVRR #8		JM-1	CM-1	OF-3	FFW-1	FFW-3	JM-3	MS-1	MB-1	OF-1
EFF 2:01 10/28/62		DAILY	DAILY	DAILY	XSUN.	TWTF	DAILY	DAILY	DAILY	DAILY
		A.M.	A.M.	P.M.	P.M.	P.M.	P.M.	P.M.	P.M.	P.M.
OAK ISLAND	LV	6.00			7.45		9.00			
RICHARDS						8.15	12.01			
EAST PENN JCT	AR				10.15	8.45	2.10			
	LV				10.30	9.15	2.30			
PACKERTON	AR	11.00			11.15	10.00	3.30			
	LV	2.00			11.30	10.20	4.30			
COXTON	AR	5.00			1.30	12.20	7.15			
	LV	6.00			1.45	12.40	8.00			
OWEGO	LV			2.30						9.45
SAYRE	AR	10.00		3.15	3.20	2.15	10.15			10.30
	LV	12.01	8.00		3.40	2.45	11.00			
MANCHESTER	AR	4.00	11.00		5.30	4.35	1.15			
	LV				5.40	6.10		3.30	4.00	
BUFFALO TIFFT	AR				7.45	8.15			7.15	
SUSP. BRIDGE	AR							6.45		
		A.M.	A.M.	P.M.	A.M.	A.M.	P.M.	P.M.	P.M.	P.M.

CNJ #18		JC 5	AC 1	JN 5	JC3	AC 3	OA 1	YA 1	OA 3	AF 1	JH 7
EFF. 2.01 10/29/61		DAILY	DAILY	DAILY	DAILY	DAILY	DAILY	EX. SU.	DAILY	DAILY	DAILY
		A.M.	A.M.	A.M.	A.M.	P.M.	P.M.	P.M.	P.M.	P.M.	P.M.
PU-PHILLIPSBURG		12.35			8.25		5.00	5.15	9.10		10.40
JU-BETHLEHEM JCT.											
STEEL-E.E.-ALLENTOWN YARD		1.10			9.00		5.30	6.15	10.00		11.29
R-EAST END-ALLENTOWN TERM.			4.00			2.40				10.00	
WK-WEST END-ALLENTOWN TERM.		1.25	4.10							10.10	
D-JIM THORPE		2.25	5.00		10.15	3.55				11.40	
PQ-NESQUEHONING JCT.		3.55	5.10	4.15	12.01					12.10	
HK-HAUCKS				5.15							
CO-PENOBSCOT			6.45							3.45	
AY-ASHLEY	AR	6.30									
	LV	6.45	7.30		3.10	8.40				4.30	
WS-WILKES-BARRE		7.15	8.15		3.55	9.45					
KF-TAYLOR		8.15	9.40		5.20	10.45					
JO-SCRANTON		8.45	10.15		5.35	11.30					
		A.M.	A.M.	A.M.	P.M.	P.M.	P.M.	P.M.	P.M.	A.M.	P.M.

Bibliography

Archer, Robert F., <u>A History of the Lehigh Valley Railroad</u>, Berkeley: Howell-North Books, 1977

Bednar, Mike, <u>Lehigh Valley Railroad - New York Division</u>, Laury's Station, Garrigues House, 1993

<u>Call-Chronicle</u>, "Heavy Storm Slows Last Passenger Run of LVRR", Allentown, Feb 4, 1961, p21

Drury, George H., <u>The Historical Guide To North American Railroads</u>, Waukesha, Kalmbach Publishing Co., 1991

Hovinen, Gary R. and Elizabeth L., <u>Pennsylvania Dutch Country</u>, Lancaster, Pennsylvania Publishers, 1986

Jahn, Richard W., "A Journey's End - CNJ & LV", <u>Flags Diamonds and Statues</u>, Vol. 10, No. 1 & 2 pp 18-43

Kulp, Randolph L., <u>Railroads In The Lehigh Valley</u>. Bethlehem, ABC Printing and Offset, 1962

Lewis, W. David, <u>Iron And Steel In America</u>, Meriden CT, The Meriden Gravure Co., 1976

Lilly, Douglas E., <u>The Lehigh and New England Railroad</u>, Laury's Station, Anthracite Railroads Historical Society / Garrigues House, 1988

Lilly, Douglas E., "Cabooses of the Lehigh & New England", <u>Flags Diamonds and Statues</u>, Vol. 6, No 1, p 40

Mentzell, Robert, <u>Northampton Borough Diamond Jubilee</u>, Northampton, R & S Printers, 1976

Parton, W. Julian, <u>The Death Of A Great Company</u>, Phillipsburg, Harmony Press, 1986

Pinkepank, Jerry A., <u>Diesel Spotters Guide</u>, Milwaukee, Kalmbach Publishing Co. 1967

Rowland, Jim, "The Lehigh and Hudson River C420's", <u>Flags Diamonds and Statues</u>, Vol. 13, No. 2, pp 23-26

Shank, William H., <u>The Amazing Pennsylvania Canals</u>, York, American Canal & Transportation Center, 1973

Wise, Robert, "A Journey's End", <u>Flags Diamonds and Statues</u>, Vol. 10, No. 1 & 2 pp 4-17

A 1960's view looking west along the CNJ right of way at mile 96. The siding runs from the Allen (Dragon) Cement Company branch to a stub-end team track at Siegfried. Originally, the sidetrack reconnected with the mainline east of 21st Street. Notice rails spiked directly to the ties and the pallet used to bridge the swampy area between the ballast and the signal box.